The Other Odyssey

The Other Odyssey

poems

Richard Garcia

Dream Horse Press
Aptos, California

Dream Horse Press
Post Office Box 2080, Aptos, California 95001-2080

Printed in the United States of America
Published in 2014 by Dream Horse Press

ISBN 978-1-935716-28-0

Cover artwork:

Lost Journey
by Bhavesh Zala
http://bhaveshzala.wordpress.com/

for Katherine

CONTENTS

With No-One to Guide Us

Between the fiery blood-stained star nursery
and the glassy edge where time crumbles

we proceeded, leaving the memory of our bodies
with only a desire for desire to pull us forward.

Dreams did not, at first, deign to follow,
but we assumed they would not be far behind.

After all, what were we, just powdery illusion,
solid enough for travel if we did not look back.

We built a place for ourselves in the night sky
at the circumference of the great wheel

knowing we would never return, but
it was something we could look forward to

that was beyond what could be imagined.
It was deer that taught us how to make a place

for ourselves in tall grass, how to circle and be still,
how to lie down in the dark, just the two of us.

Offbeat Museums

In the Museum of Regrets
you can ride into the Tunnel of Regrets.
Over the entrance is a giant clock
that is always set at 3 AM.

In the Museum of Lost Objects
You can enter the Room of Lost Objects.
There is one of Amelia Earhart's shoes.
Hemingway's suitcase.

In the Museum of Songs You Can't Remember
you can listen to songs you can't remember.

The Museum of Clothespins
is but a small section
of the Museum of Fasteners.
Not much to see really,
metal clothespins, plastic clothespins.
Early prototypes made of bone.
Bigger than a stepladder,
the world's largest clothespin.

The Museum of Missed Moments.
The Museum of the Unborn.
The Museum of Ice.
The Museum of Sounds Heard in the Night.
The Museum of the Insulted.

Too many to see in one day.
In the cafeteria of the Museum of Dawn
be sure to try the slice of yellow light
served on a deep-blue platter.

Museums and Questions

In the Museum of Dog Barks
You can listen to dog barks
from all over the world.
They even have the wheezing
of the dingo, which does not bark.

Did you know that George Washington
lost a sock at the Battle of Ticonderoga?
There it is, on display, after being purchased
from the British Military Museum for an undisclosed sum,
at The Museum of Lost Things.

How long will honey last in a pyramid?

How long will a human heart last
in a jar of Tupelo honey?
What famous author was embalmed
in a barrel of honey and brought home
on a sailing ship from what faraway island?

What does the body remember?

My feet remember being the last of me
to be born. Are my feet younger than my head?
You might as well ask, Does music have a soul.

In the Museum of Souls, in Last Chance, Tennessee,
souls are on display in mason jars. Of course,
they are invisible, but the hand-written labels
explain which soul is in which jar.

Why are coconuts hairy?

Is coconut milk really milk?
Has anyone escaped from Devils Island
floating on a raft made of coconuts?
Can a coconut drift around the world?
How many people have been killed
by falling coconuts? Can coconuts
form an island? Have secret messages
of great importance been concealed inside coconuts?
You can learn the answers to these questions
and more in the Museum of Coconuts.

The Museum of Lost Single Socks

In the Museum of Lost Single Socks
you can find the missing socks of Genghis Khan.

Genghis Khan had many socks especially woven
for quick removal because he had so many wives.
He may have had more wives than horses.

He is said to have mounted at least three wives a day.
For each he would wear a new outfit
so it is no wonder that he lost so many socks.

No one loses two socks. Two socks lost
is simply missing laundry. But one sock?
The void of the forever incomplete.
The mystery of unexplained disappearance.

In the Museum of Lost Single Socks
there is a room full of unusual socks.
A single chain-mail sock lost by a crusader.
A single sock made of human skin
that was lost by Vlad the Impaler.

Ladies take note: A single sock with a rock
knotted into its toe, carried in your purse,
is a formidable weapon.

Polar explorers do not get lost
until they lose one sock. After that
they limp and wander in circles.

If it is the left sock that they lose
they wander to the left. A right sock
and they will circle clockwise.

Soon they think that they are burning up
in tropical heat, they throw off all their clothes,
lie down, and rub snow over their chests.

Having just one sock on can be erotic.
That is why thirty-five percent of the world's population
is descended from Genghis Khan.

In Mongolian, 'Genghis Khan' is not a name
but a title. It means One Sock, or He of the Missing Sock.

Music for Airports

To those transfixed in the tunnel of colored lights
To those frozen on the escalators
below constellations of candles
wreathed in the cascade of didgeridoo vibrations
and the wet clicking of tree frogs.

Please bring your lost items to the lost and found.

The peninsula will be become an island.

The Northwest Passage will open its chest
offering us the fossilized bones of explorers.

Observe out the window over the starboard wing:
the residue of the meteor that killed the dinosaurs.

Devil's Slide, the Devil's Highchair, the Devil's Post Office.

Stops at Rock Creek Illinois, Rock Creek California,
Rock Creek Colorado, Rock Creek Kansas, Rock Creek Utah
and Rock Creek Park in Washington DC have been cancelled.

Federal law prohibits dreaming past midnight.
Passengers showing signs of REM activity
will be shaken awake and asked
one of those questions that have no answer.

Beware of well-dressed, well-mannered strangers.

Pay no attention to the stewardess
who walks in stiff skin down the aisle.

She cannot see or hear you.
That is why she whispers to no-one in particular:
Please don't touch my body, please,
don't touch my body.

The Boxes

The islanders woke up to find that during the night
the tide deposited thousands of boxes on the shore.
The islanders rushed to the shore as word spread.

The first box contained a teddy bear the chief had lost.
The second box contained something someone had borrowed.
The third box was so beautifully wrapped no-one would open it.

Objects in each box were transformed when they were removed.
Thus a toy jeep, circa 1941, became a Jeep Cherokee.
A tiny walkie-talkie became a cell phone.

They knew that there would not be time to open all the boxes.
Henceforth, the priest would include boxes in all his sermons.
He said: a coffin is a box. You are a box. Hell is a box,

but Heaven is a box that only Christ can open.
Years later, the beach was still littered with boxes.
The remains of the boxes drifted out to sea.

The village was not big enough to contain the boxes.
In gratitude the villagers enclosed the village in a gigantic box.
On the closed lid they painted the sky and the constellations.

On the first interior wall they painted the mountains.
On the second, trees of the forest, and the creatures.
On the third wall they painted cliffs, waterfalls, birds

and rainbows. On the fourth wall they painted the ocean.
Barely visible in the distance, the flotillas of discarded boxes
drifting away from the shore like a retreating armada.

The White Ghosts

White ghosts were ruining the neighborhood
like an army of blank real estate signs,
like refrigerators abandoned on front lawns
that were really graveyards.
This occurred to me while I took a shower
with the sister of my former wife.
She was so afraid of the white ghosts,
she wore her bathing suit
and over that, her dark blue dress.
I wrote this down on her dress
with a pen that had white waterproof ink.
I wanted to write more about the white ghosts
so I peeled her dress off.
She liked that and kissed me,
sticking her tongue into my mouth.
Her tongue was not soft and warm
but stiff and cool like cardboard,
and tasted like a communion wafer.
Then I lay next to you thinking,
it's good I brought her dress with me
so I could write about the white ghosts.
Then I thought, you fool, you can't carry
things out of a dream, so forget about
the white ghosts. I got up and took
my dog to the park but he would not
get out of the car. I don't know for sure,
but I think the field was full of white ghosts,
and he could see them standing there,
silent, like the ghosts of a Ku Klux Klan meeting.
White noise is not white.

White chocolate is not chocolate.
Avalanches are not soft and fluffy.
When I got home, the ghost
of a white pit bull was writhing
on the kitchen floor, whining and sliding
toward me across the linoleum on her belly.

A Test to Determine if You Have Extraterrestrial Ancestry

Has a dead bird ever fallen out of the sky
and landed at your feet
when you were quarreling with a girlfriend?

While standing in a shallow stream
has a large fish swum around your knees
three times as if in salutation?

Have you ever dreamt an entire
lifetime in a few moments of deep sleep?
Did you wake feeling sad?

Have you ever seen stars sliding
across the entire sky? Have you heard
your name spoken when you were alone?

Do you like to touch fuzzy objects?
If you watch a boxing match, do you
identify with the winner or the loser?

During a job interview would you remark
How sad that Kiki, darling of Montmartre,
mistress of Man Ray, had absolutely no pubic hair?

When you enter a room full of strangers,
do you get an immediate foreknowledge
that you are about to be insulted?

if you are invited to a wedding do you think:
A: You are a guest of honor?
B: You will be asked to recite a poem about your dog?
C: None of the above?

And finally, when you read the phrase, "none of the above," did you seem to remember that there is a place you can't remember?

Japanese Scientists

Japanese scientists unveil a robot that plays the violin.
I read this sentence to you as we lie in bed.
I wonder, does it play *Bach's Partita in G minor* so beautifully,
butterflies on migration plunge into the sea
and the moon takes a drink of sadness mixed with gin?
You're too sleepy to answer. Our dog lies down between us.
Now I'm reading another but I think you can't hear me.
Japanese scientists unveil a robot that solves Rubik's Cube.
I look over at you. No reaction. Our dog. No reaction.
Japanese scientists unveil a robot that dances the Blue Danube.
I'm on the edge of the bed, my feet are cold. I nudge our dog.
He growls at me in his sleep. Just then, Japanese scientists
unveil a robot snowplow that eats snow and excretes ice logs.
I put on my special sleep mask, also made by Japanese scientists.
Cold air shoots into my nose, a hand of cold air presses against
my tongue and holds my throat open. I turn off the light
and descend into an abandoned tunnel; scent of ozone
and creosote, crunch of gravel, concrete and railroad tracks.
I have wasted the day; now I wander the night alone.
Meanwhile Japanese scientists unveil a robot exoskeleton
that can be worn by elderly farmers. Japanese scientists
unveil a robot that walks on the command of a monkey
running on a treadmill in North Carolina. Japanese scientists.

Trout Dreams

A trout stream appears in the street
and you find a fly rod
leaning against a lamppost,
all set to go with a light tippet
and a royal humpy.

You are on the moon
and your dog is barking
at the earth.
It is so large
against the moon's horizon.
It is a good thing
you are both wearing
your space helmets.

You and your cellmate Frank
argue over whose dream it is.
Frank—in for double murder,
a.k.a. Philadelphia Lawyer—
so convincing, and you wonder,
if it is his dream, where will
you go when he wakes up?

You are driving in your convertible.
You turn on the radio:
it is you reading a poem
about riding on the back
of an enormous leaping trout.

An enormous leaping trout—
you can barely hang on.
Yippee ki-yay
under the full moon.

There you are in the LA Times:
lying on your belly
in the surf wearing
your black cowboy hat.
Katherine is there, pulling
hard on a bent fly rod.
The fly line is clenched in your teeth.

Yes, April is the cruelest month
and April first is the cruelest day.
You turn on the radio again—
it is the muffled static,
the faraway, barely audible
barking of your dog.

String Theory

When an angel has been bad
it has to sit in a corner of the universe
wearing the dunce cap of string theory.

An angel blows on a trumpet
and its high, golden light reflects
the spider web of string theory.

When Adam first saw himself
reflected in Eve's eyes
he thought of string theory.

The secret of string theory
is contained somewhere
in the world's largest ball of string,

which can be found in Darwin, Minnesota
on display in The Pavilion of String Theory.
It is guarded by a six-foot-tall hinged man.

He is called the Guardian of String Theory.
When an angel has a bad day
it sits in a corner of the universe

and contemplates string theory.
It might even pluck a string or two.
A plucked string oscillates between worlds.

Somewhere a man looks up from his desk
at the Department of Motor Vehicles
while thinking of string theory,

sees a woman he does not know is
the sister of his future wife, and all
because of string theory, speaks to her.

Mammatus Clouds over Hastings, Nebraska

after a photo by Jorn Olsen

Yonder clouds, 'tis like the sky
is filled with teats,
milk dripping down instead of rain,
greenish-blue milk, warm, slightly sweet.

And then there are the neo-colonial clouds
taking their leave of the remains of empire
not needed now that the natives observe teatime.

Let's not talk about those ocean clouds
that sizzle along the horizon when the sun sinks.
Drama queens, all of them. What kind of clouds
will welcome my last day—one-way clouds
run out of destination, or will they be clouds
of memory not remembered by anyone?

Yonder cloud, 'tis shaped something like a…

but then again maybe not. Some clouds
are curtains pulled around hospital beds.
Some clouds are so heavy they fall
and land on the earth like gigantic spider webs.

Needing to distract the sentry,
I remark on how that cloud is like
a pair of garden shears left out overnight
on a plastic table in a backyard surrounded by bamboo.

The sentry, sensing that I am trying to slip by him
and perhaps shimmy down the parapets of dawn,

replies, No, I think that cloud
looks more like a palpitating, phosphorescent cord
that bears a strong resemblance
to the intestines of a disemboweled traitor
strewn across the cobblestones by dogs.

Self Portrait with *Two Fridas*

One Richard reaches to tap his back pocket
to be sure he still has his wallet.

One Frida looks calm, although her heart
is hanging outside of her body.

One Richard appears to be melting.

The other Frida fiddles with a thimble
held between her fingers.

One Richard is a lifelong practitioner
of the art of invisibility.

The other Richard looks old, harmless,
but carries a concealed weapon.

Blue dress Frida.
White dress Frida.

One dress stained with blood.
A hemostat clamps the one artery
both Fridas share.

One Richard standing in line at the bank.
The other seeping into the ground
in an empty lot, behind an abandoned supermarket.

White dress Frida.
Blue dress Frida.
Both holding hands.

A dress for dancing.
A dress to be buried in.

One Richard tells the other Richard
You are the sky that wants so much to rain.
One Frida tells the other Frida,
You are the sky that wants so much to rain.

Mystical Journey with Commands

We were an ill-sorted fellowship.
Clyde the punch-drunk ex-boxer.
Melody the classical muse.
A talking dog that would not reveal his name.
Assorted lollygaggers and pathetic miscreants.
Our ship sailed at dawn.
No not a ship but the house
I grew up in, outfitted with sails.
Occasionally a loudspeaker hidden in the sky
barked out commands:
Hey you kids, get offa that roof!
The talking dog talked in his sleep.
As we rowed toward our ship
a flying fish landed in my lap.
Not a flying fish, a silver coin.
I stuck it in the pocket of my pantaloons
knowing it would come in handy some day.
Move away from the vehicle!
A ship's bell clanged, once, twice,
and Clyde stood up and began to box
with the air, almost upsetting our boat
until the talking dog mimicked another bell
and Clyde sat down in the stern.
Do not be alarmed. This is only a test.
At that rate we arrived at the ship
by midnight, but the tide had risen again
and we were ready for adventure.
Days passed in the Horse Latitudes.
Nights passed in the Doldrums of Lassitude.
By accident, we came upon the kelp highway

and set a course for the New World.
Melody, the classical muse, who
had been as quiet as a statue, spoke:
If this were a real poem, there would be music.
Thus it was we drifted off the coast
of the singing dunes of Zanzibar.
Thus it was we came to an island
that seemed to be sleeping.
But I won't bore you anymore
with tedious details of our journey:
the rescued girl-child that was really
an excommunicated wizard,
the ghosts hungry for a drop of lizard blood,
the sands, sighing as they cooled in the evening,
the harmonics of the aurora borealis.
On the Beach of the Sleeping Island
we came upon a curious crowd of early arrivals
milling around, scratching their heads, bewildered.
All right people, back off, move along,
there's nothing for you to see here!

Dangerous Journeys and the Wizard of Oz

One kept a knife in his boot.
A truck was completely handmade.
We made love in a ditch in Texas.
Woke up parked on the railroad tracks.

When Dorothy opens the door
and sees Oz for the first time.

A truck was completely handmade.
One swallowed pills to stay awake.
Woke up parked on the railroad tracks.
Officer, I already have a ticket for that.

From sepia-toned to brilliant color.

One swallowed pills to stay awake.
Missed a turn, plunged down an embankment.
Officer, I already have a ticket for that.
Peggy's small arms around my waist.

Giggles in the bushes are munchkins.

Missed a turn, plunged down an embankment.
Crossed the bridge on my bike, 110 MPH.
Peggy's head, nestled against my back.
A bear did body work on my Volvo.

What makes the Hottentots so hot?

Missed a turn, plunged down an embankment.
I forgot the gas can was hidden under the hood.
A bear did body work on my Volvo.
One kept a knife in his boot.

There's no place like home, there's no place like home.

Either/Or and Favorite Movies

Either the bandolier or the blue mascot,
either the chevalier or the grey ascot.

Either the stock market's in a panic
or *The Chambermaid on the Titanic*.

Either Laurel and Hardy in *Way Out West*
or pulling a crazy in your boss's office.

Either stepping on the fire ants' tiny volcano
or the man behind the curtain's a no-show.

Either target practice in the shooting gallery
or the long, long-take bank robbery.

Either the buttercups and purple butterflies
or the hat brim and the scalloped bowtie.

Either curled up on the couch all afternoon
or the shelving collapses like the stroke of doom.

Either a fat man and a skinny man dancing tippy-toes
or down in the boonies where the postman doesn't go.

Either Aha! you exclaim, Profound coincidence,
or a cappella Ellington in *The Harmonists*.

Either Annie Laurie slipping nylons over her thighs
Or you're chugging a Guinness, one of the guys.

Either Yojimbo gets his sword back
or Dr. Zhivago has a heart attack.

Either there goes Lara, love of your life,
or there goes Lara, love of your life.

Complete Guide to Los Angeles County

He's memorized the *Complete Guide.*
He's eight years old.
He will never be lost.
Listens to traffic on the radio.

He's eight years old.
Walks through the building.
Listens to traffic on the radio.
Staring at his feet.

Walks through the building.
Best way to the airport?
Staring at his feet,
Don't take the freeway,

best way to the airport
Lincoln all the way there.
Can you draw us an animal?
Draws a FedEx box.

Lincoln all the way there.
Draws a skyline of buildings.
Draws a FedEx box
Signs sticking out of the buildings.

Draws a skyline of buildings.
Radiology Dialysis Security
Signs sticking out of the buildings.
All the signs he passed today.

Radiology Dialysis Security.
Time for bed, Mom reads from the guide.
All the signs he passed today.
Good night 10, Goodnight Pico.

Time for bed, Mom reads from the guide.
Good night 405, goodnight Sepulveda.
Good night 10, Goodnight Pico.
He dreams he's sitting on the moon.

Good night 405, goodnight Sepulveda.
It's okay, he's got the *Complete Guide*.
He dreams he's sitting on the moon.
Beyond the grey horizon, Earth rises.

It's okay, he's got the *Complete Guide*.
It's so nice and quiet now.
Beyond the grey horizon, Earth rises.
He will never be lost.

Down

Seventh floor, Rooftop, Enchanted Forest.
Please watch your step.

Wrong floor, says Mr. Crow.
Behind a frowning tree
we find the way

and down we go.
Sixth floor, Garden Supplies.
Do not attempt to sit on the railing.

Men's Sportswear, Teen Spirit,
Toys for the Little Ones…
I'd like to get off. Not yet,

says Mr. Crow. Ladies Wear,
Lingerie, girdles, panties,
panty girdles, slips, garters,
slippers with golden tassels…

I close my eyes. Look,
Says Mr. Crow. I open my eyes—
across on the up escalator

a boy who looks exactly
like me. Caw-caw,
the velvet crow

on his shoulder. Caw-
caw, caws back Mr. Crow.
Mezzanine, Ladies Lounge,

Powder Room. First floor. Base-
ment. Employees only. Please
watch your step.

Look, says Mr. Crow, flapping in the dark.
This is where they grow the dolls. See,
such tiny yellow fingers poking out of the dirt.

Thomas

I washed my veins
and hung them out to dry.
My neighbors complained,
called me trailer-trash:
No-one uses a clothesline anymore.

I placed one stone on top of another stone.
It was not a black stone on a white stone
or a white stone on a black stone
and I did not know if it was raining.

I wanted to mark a path
I could not return on.

I vowed not to move until you came my way again.

Then I remembered that you were last seen
riding a black horse across a crater on the moon.
It was a small crater with a common first name.
Thomas I think, or just Tom.

For the next several years I followed a stone
I dropped into a well.
I was the well.
I became the stone.

Now my hands are all that is left of me.
I don't really need the rest.

Except for my eyes. They tell me
they can see right through my hands.

Harry Gamble

We laughed when, like a fop he saw in a movie,
he pulled a handkerchief from his sleeve,
swished it around and said, My dear fellow.

He came to see me before he left for 'Nam.
He dropped by, but I was not there.
He left a number I never called.

I still see him from time to time. Everywhere.

Spring

I dreamed I was looking at a poem on a computer screen.
A prosaic poem based on a photograph of the plotters

of Lincoln's assassination. It must have been the program
on Lincoln's death and the hunt for the guilty on PBS.

The poem was in nine unrhymed couplets. It did not seem odd
that the images in the photograph were also the words.

Nine conspirators sitting in chairs. One was a woman, rather
matronly. It seemed to be early spring, a dust of snow

on the ground. It looked cold. The plotters wore lots of clothes.
Did I press the wrong button? A couplet vanished from the screen.

But the chair remained. A young man sauntered up to it
and sat down. His trucker's cap was on backwards. He wore

a plaid shirt and large unlaced sneakers. He unwrapped
a hamburger and began to eat. He waved his hamburger

in the direction of the photographer. He laughed,
but there was no sound. Then it was as if someone

yelled at him. Sheepishly, he wandered off. The missing couplet
popped back onto the page. The title of the poem was, Spring.

Saudade

They call it fall but I see the leaves
rising into the air, spinning, spun about.
Lucifer fell or was he thrown, flung, pushed?
Maybe pieces of galaxies came tumbling with him

as I fell last night, crashing through rooftops.
It seems I had done something completely wrong.
Something that seemed right at the time,
like turning a would-be lover into a friend.

Each rooftop was a life. Each house,
a lifetime. I did right as far as this world,
but in the eternal? No! some angel-types shouted,
You idiot! And they pushed me

through the floor and sent me crashing,
smashing rooftops, living rooms, foundations.
What a racket, no wonder I woke up.
Was this the last of my rooms?

I lay on a bed, afraid to open my eyes.
One hand was on my chest, about
where my heart should be. The other,
pressed hard against a curtain and wall.

OK. I was human. In a room. On a bed.
I opened my eyes. You were still asleep,
undisturbed by any crash-landings.
The window above my hand was open.

Ah yes, fall. Windows open. No heat, no bugs.
So I lay there, slowly remembering where I was.
But missing, terribly, someone or something.
But I did not know who, or what.

Susan Falling

When you writhe
to the occasion,
perhaps it's Mississippi
Delta meets
the Goddess Kali
in Katmandu, your
cry of painful bliss
brighter than
the first light bulb
which I understand
still flickers
in the Museum
of Light in Sue
Falls, Idaho,
named of course
after you, and
your famous falling.
Susan, I say,
is your name
really Susan,
and is it
your falling
that sticks to time
and rips
a tiny tear
in its netted stocking?
O tearful moaning
after the foolish moon,
you are more
than the geyser

of exclamation forcing
its way through
the brambles
of my never-after
life, life
ghost-written
by an impatient ghost.
And the hand
that shakes the dice
comes up chicken bones
in the medicine cabinet.
When I reach
to catch your body
I fall with you
into the wrinkles
of light and rain,
the rain and its shivering drums.

Falling Pattern

Thoughts are falling,
intergalactic thoughts,
falling through the roof
into our bodies.
They don't make noise
so we think they are
our own thoughts.
They stand inside our bodies
and borrow our vision,
peering out of our eyes.
That is the only way
they can see what we call
the world. They are intrigued
since they know nothing of time
or happenstance.
Katherine, I say to you
although your name is Linda,
What are you thinking?
Nothing you say
because right now a thought
is inside you
peering out of the amber
kaleidoscope of your eyes.
Katherine of the steppes,
of the plateau rising out of
a jungle where no man
has set foot. Katherine
who says we are floating.
No, we're falling, I say,
Falling in a pattern. And

happenstance, what
is that but us,
the way we happen
to stand across
from each other
making a kind of bridge
with our glances,
a spiral staircase
with a waxy banister
for the falling thoughts
to come sliding down
into our thoughts.

Louise

Louise of the black
skirt, black stockings,
checkered apron: the
Waffle House Story
could be our story.
Louise, always in a hurry.
Not noticing when I place
the dishes in the Hobart
in columns of five,
how they march
into the steaming maw
like history. The Waffle
House Fun Facts could
be our Waffle House
fun facts—how
many kisses in a life-
time laid end to end
from Georgia to Ca-
lifor-ni-ay and back
seven times? It is I,
speaking to you, Louise,
I with the thick
rubber gloves, up
to my elbows in pots,
here to say, Louise,
Waffle House Boogie
could be our song.
I am standing on
a milk crate, stirring
soapy water

in the soup kettle
with a wooden ladle,
I am falling off the milk
crate as you wander by.
Sweat drips
from my paper hat
to my apron. And
I am nothing
but a grill-brick,
good for nothing
but being shoved back
and forth across a warm
greasy grill. But even if,
as I have heard it said,
your name is not Louise,
Louise, can you hear deep
within the hum of the dishwashing
machine, one of those quiet moments
in the storm of a Beethoven quartet?
Listen, the snow flurry
subsides, and our troika
pulled by white horses
comes to rest in a clearing.

Tumbling

You with your mouth of honky-tonk
and day-glow laughter,
your tongue of Jack Daniels,
of feather in the dark,

your death-defying candles,
and brooding brow
of a statue buried in sand.
Your waist makes me sad.

I declare certain curvatures
were devised by the devil
on the seventh day
of creation. Your sidelong

glance of incendiary icebergs
makes me forget my name.
Your hair is copper-plated, ready
for battle. Your hips sway

like Rita Hayworth in a silver
lamé evening gown, singing
Put the Blame on Me Boys.
The prow of your elbow

cleaves through breakers of sleep,
your sleep where the skeletons of angels
with brittle, transparent wings,
are tumbling out of the sky.

Gacela of Grey Stone

Grey stone, let there be a pact between us,
your ire flashing, searing the wind,
my leave-taking of matters best left.

I want the silken fuchsia in the pewter vase.
No, not that, but the way it sings
when it sings only to itself.

Remember when we scaled
the sandstone cliffs of longing,
your midnight mascara, my bandolier?

I don't want to be the collateral damage
of leftover fire fights and skirmishes.
I want the explosion turned inside-out

revealing its chilly, hardened core.
I want to spy your fingers
strumming spider webs of woven steel.

Gacela of Noon

I want a constellation without shadow.
I want a crystalline wafer melting on my tongue.
I want poison ivy to spring from my wrists,
chimes of midday to herald the white raven.

I do not want the obsidian mirror
or its reflected smoke to obliterate dawn.
I refuse to kiss the cold pebble
as it sinks to the bottom of my sleep.

Remember the year my fingerprints
were stapled to the wind?
Remember when your shapeliness
made the tide change its mind?

I want to step into the stairwell of my throat
and follow the rumor of my footsteps.
For my heart is littered with machinery
left over from the industrial apocalypse.

Gacela of the Mutant Jellyfish

I want to be a bubble trapped in amber,
a million-year comma, a parenthesis.
I don't want to be a sugar container full of gravel
hidden in a house about to be destroyed.

The President sits reading on the toilet:
Giant Jellyfish Attacks America.
¡Aí Diós mío! the president exclaims,
reaching for the toilet paper.

No one sees that the jellyfish resembles a brain
decorated with flowing dreadlocks of rocket smoke.
No one sees the mutant jellyfish advance
on the replica of Small Town, USA,

its frothy feet a churning wave.
I want to be a bubble trapped in amber,
a million-year comma, a parenthesis,
an ellipsis hiding within a cocoon of silence.

I don't want to be inside the wave
with the manikins dressed up like Mom and Dad.
Inside the wave with the chimpanzee
strapped to a crib, the family dog, its bone.

Gacela of the Sheet of Paper

Not the sheet of paper rolled into a tight cone,
dipped into a paste of flour and water,
sharpened against a scrap of emery board.

But one that waits patiently to be folded.
The one crumpled up into a ball, or dancing, like
those sheets of paper observed by the first aviators
revolving in the currents of clouds.

Aí, Luna, goddess of paper, unroll your mantle:
did you not glisten the skin of my first love
just before her mother came home
from the graveyard shift at Can-Co
and I slipped out the window, seen only
by you and the paperboy?

Not the spear made of paper, flicked
from a notch in a pencil between prison bars,
across tiers and rampways, the one
that can pierce a man's heart.

Without significance, wet paper in the rain.
The birth certificate, the death certificate,
the warrant, the summons, the sealed orders.

I want that sheet of paper slipped under a door
at midnight, that code invisible to all but candle flame.

Gacela of the Wanting

What does the gazelle want?
It wants to romance the earthworm.

What do the ants want?
They want to find their way back
to the sleeping child's house.

The wind has searched for you
and returned with nothing but leafy smoke
in its little silver box.

The moon, what about the moon?
The moon staggers
over the cobblestones.

Open your eyes, corpse—
the moon is calling you
from the heart of the pomegranate.

Look at your hand.
Just look at your hand.
It is no longer yours to give away.

What is the opposite of desire?
Nothing, nothing is the opposite of desire.

Fugue of the Open Hand

The open hand reaches for something.
Something, another hand, reaches for a map.
Lifeline, love line, crossroads.
Four men in cloaks standing on a hill.

Something, a hand, reaches for a map.
But no map leads backwards.
Four men in cloaks, standing on a hill.
Below, a small whale, stranded on the beach.

No map leads backwards.
The thumb stands apart, sullen Napoleon.

The future trembles in the rain.
Constellations drift over steeples.
The thumb stands apart, sullen Napoleon.
There are no bodies in dreams, only hands.

Constellations drift over steeples.
Lifeline, love line, crossroads.
There are no bodies in the future.
There are no bodies in the future.

What is the difference between a cloak
and a cape? Both take a certain panache.

How about a glove and a mitten?
A hand and the fin of a whale?
An open hand and a claw?
A fist and a club?

I did not know who I was
until I could point to what I was not.
The one I was, the many I was not.
The hand is a map. The map is a mirror.
What do you see? Two hands.
Two hands cradling fire.

A Play for Finger Puppets in Five Acts

The fingers want to run away and join the circus.
Thumb says Stay put. He's so fat.

No future here, only backward.
One cloak for each finger.
We need some things in here besides cloaks,
like an African jar, a potted tulip,
Spanish doubloons, a thermos,
a wooden clock, a clam shell,
and a clothesline tossed over a wall.

Thumb says I can make the ears of the donkey.
Hand says I can latch wings together.

Fingers say We can be an old man's eye
and the tassels on his cockscomb hat.
Better yet, we can all be crabs coming out of holes in the sand.
Hand, check the mailbox. Behave yourself. Don't point knives.

Imagine two white gloves against a black velvet background.
One glove is named Marsha. The other is named John.
Marsha says Oh John. John says Oh Marsha.
Oooooh John. Oh, oh, oh, Marsha. And so on.

A Poem by Kit Loney

Even though scientists
have found the bones of time,
I can still draw cats
or palmetto bugs,
which is one way of saying
cockroach, even if
I'm only jump-roping
on a gravel driveway.
Even though I am not
Kit Loney, I can still
write this, my first poem
by Kit Loney. After all,
time is slowing down
just as surely as tired
shadows drag their feet.
A cat sits on a lawn,
the curve of her whiskers
makes her appear to be smiling.
But when she runs, she runs
on the wind, she runs on the wind.
I can draw a straw
that turns out to be
my real name, Katherine,
which comes from Grandfather's
lover. No, not the one
in Alaska who claimed
not to know he was married.
I can draw myself
racing down a hill
on my bike, Flash.

But what did I know?
It was midnight, July
'67, and I refused to wear
my training bra because
I thought my blue floppy hat
flapping in the wind
made me a hippie.
But even then I suspected
the caboodle of time,
like a dryer in the Open-
All-Night Laundromat,
was slowing down slowing
down. I could tell by the way
the spokes of my bicycle
flickered backwards in slow motion,
in the light of the silver moon.
In the light of the silver moon.

A Poem by Andy Rooney

How about these paperclips?
Consider the humble paperclip.
Paperclips do not like to remain in their containers.
Paperclips can be found at the bottom of the sea.
The first paperclip was made of mastodon ivory.
Some paperclips are covered in plastic.
Some paperclips are plastic.
Metal paperclips are desirable.
You can twist them while on the phone.
You can use one to pick your teeth.
It is not recommended to use a paperclip to pick your teeth.
A paperclip can unlock a handcuff.
A paperclip cannot unlock a plastic handcuff.
Last time I mentioned paperclips
I received boxes of paperclips in the mail.
Here are some candy paperclips.
You can use them to attach important papers together.
You can eat the candy paperclips.
Paperclips are like some marriages.
They clip things together temporarily.
Please don't send me any more paperclips.
You can use paperclips to brush your eyebrows.
It is a little known fact, but every computer
has a secret tiny hole somewhere on its body
into which you can insert a straightened paperclip.
Usually, a frozen computer will start up again
when you insert the unfolded paperclip into its tiny, secret hole.
Your IT guy at the office would rather you did not know
about the tiny, secret paperclip hole in your computer.
Paperclips have been sprinkled into space by scientists.
Paperclips ring the planet. Some planets have rings of ice,

boulders, bits of exploded comet, purple and yellow meteor dust.
Our planet has a ring of millions of paperclips.
Recently it had been noticed that the paperclips
are joining together, each clip attaching to each clip
forming a paperclip chain in the ionosphere.
Maybe mankind could learn something from all
the paperclips that have fallen into remote corners of our offices.
Here are some biodegradable paperclips made of recycled paper.
Here are some paperclips make of compressed diamond dust.
Here is a paperclip I have carried in my pocket since 1944.
It saved my life at Omaha Beach by deflecting a sniper's bullet.
As you can see, they don't make paperclips like they used too.

Double Trouble

At once I discovered the secret aleph, brain abuzz.
But did I mean it, or was I just being silly?
Could I become a comet? A ghostly aviatrix?
Dreaming of switching places with you, I felt hollow.
Even now becoming you I missed you, Luv,
for here's the rub: if I could be you,
gin would flow from King Tut's tit.
Here is where I'd say my goodbyes,
I'd say Adios, later baby, au revoir.
Just now, I'm watching my own I.Q.—
kind of like watching street lights droop.
Letting my ego dissolve into goo,
molding like alphabet soup on a futon.
Not the color gold, not the crack of chin against rim—
only backlogged light stumbling like a beginner angel.
Plodding into morning, stuttering with plink and plonk,
quashing dreamy cobwebs I quaffed my O.J.
remembering my dream of an anti-haji-
soldier in double trouble, double Dutch.
The crippled dawn limped like a three-legged dog.
Upwind and down the alley I strolled, aloof,
verily, unencumbered, even then I moved alone—
what I missed in you long-gone, abandoned.
X marked your absence of scrambled acrostic.
Why recall a story of a busted light bulb?
Zero and zero add up to one in your reverse algebra.

Escape from New York

A cold Fifth Avenue night is still a cold night
as you, moved by a story you tell yourself once again,
submit your icy fingers for evidence
to the corona of the evening moon, ringed in omen
like a puff of cocaine on a glass table.
As if New York were a pillow of drowsy smolders.
As if New York were a strobe of various vrooms.
This is the point in the poem where a passerby
might stop to admire the alliteration of smoky light
behind the window display at Juicy Couture, and note
the taste of ash in the air that nestles into his tongue.
Of course when I say you, I mean me, me running
across a rooftop, me attempting to land quietly
on the top of a truck parked in an alley.
Athena, I could fucking use a little help here—
if this time I do complete my famous *Escape
from New York*, in which the author recounts
various adventures and escapades, and which reveals
the identity of the Knight of Mirrors, and other misfortunes
that occurred concerning the absence of a certain lady
in the tavern favored by poets and literati called After Closing.
But this time New York is a frozen national park,
and the poetry prompts of billy clubs make no sound
against creamy puffs of snow, against a word frozen in mid-air—
entirely like a secret. Entirely like something you forgot
as you metamorphosed once again from a me into a third person.
The person that hears a door collapsing from kicks
of a posse intent on his extinguishing. But he is splitting
the scene, as they say, opening his eyes in another century,
as if New York was a pillow of drowsy smolders.

I Was Not

I was not that creature begging to be absolved.
I was not for lack of want.
I was not all open ears to the sea,
nor was I pastiche of mellifluous languor.

I was not for lack of want,
wanting last year's tongue gilded to my shoulder.
I was not all open ears to the sea
believing every wavely rumor

wanting last year's tongue gilded to my shoulder.
I was not García y Vega, García Lorca or Márquez,
believing every wavely rumor,
every new fucking secret corona.

I was not García y Vega, García Lorca or Márquez,
I was never myself but a story, perhaps a lullaby,
not every new fucking secret corona.
I was not some long-frozen street or avenue.

I was never myself but a story, perhaps a lullaby—
something soothing, rustle of velvet curtains against darkness.
I was not some long-frozen street or avenue.
I was not another street light extinguished,

something soothing, rustle of velvet curtains against darkness.
I was not the diminishing sound of footsteps.
I was not another street light extinguished.
I was not that creature begging to be absolved.

The Only Story I Know

I stole another woman's only scarf.
A man bought me some steak and I thought I
would let him, at least only
this once. I borrowed, OK, I stole
my husband's poems written in a woman's
voice and intended not for me, but another.

I stole my name, but that's another
story. I stole a pumpkin pie and scarfed
it up in my car while reading his poems in a woman's
voice, apparently by his other self as he says, Not I.
But how strange that these poems he stole
were written by me, yes, myself only.

My husband could purloin my poems only
because I had not written them yet. Another
thing, let me tell you, this soul-stealer stole—
Some of my best dreams, my memories, a scarf,
my joie de vivre, my very being and my glass eye.
So can you blame me if I stole another woman's

scarf another woman's scarf another woman's…
In it I was transformed into this beautiful one-and-only.
Even now I do not believe it, that I
could become someone else, yes, another,
even my husband's mistress, she of the stolen scarf.
Since he could steal even unwritten poems I also stole.

I stole his lover's identity, I stole and stole,
her teeth her smile her wedding ring all that woman's
bras panties hankies her expensive scarf,
supposedly her one scarf her only,
and I took one last thing from her, another
scarf. For if someone knows a lie, it is I.

I
stole
another
woman's
only
scarf.

This is the only story I know. A cold night, a woman's
garment. Supposedly that I stole. But I only
wanted to be another. My husband's lover with the lovely scarf.

Red Wing

Last evening only the color gold could keep me away from you,
Little Redwing. Last night's helium dreams sizzled on my tongue
as December extinguished itself in fretless smoke. I was not the
only somnambulist I knew. I remembered the fear of first light.
I was drowsy and the wind was long. Pardon me, I said, I am
ceasing to exist. I was backlogged and out of stock, my tongue
of fondue, my tongue of fondness. Absolving from room to
room I did go, searching for you Red Wing, dear exploded dust,
strobing little meteor.

After

After the war of the shipping clerks,
after the world-wide shortage of string,
after the buzz saw divided morning from itself
and daylight jumped out of dawn,

after green visors were all the rage,
after I ate lunch each day in the business park
where I waited for the white hart
to come bounding, pursued by hounds,

after there was silence on the morning of that day—
not real silence, because a car shifted gears
on the road across the marsh, after the tree frogs
took advantage of the leaves' distraction to wax electrical,

after the black hole sipped the earth's oxygen,
and we all grew taller
and my head distanced itself from my feet
and the ocean stood up on its hind legs—

but no, forget all that, this was after,
after one hundred noes your final yes like a trapdoor,
after the police broke up the party
and we were too tired to resist harbingers of the 21st century,

after the end of the world, after long ago,
after tears and corned beef in Canter's Deli,
a cavalcade of abandoned terraces and gazebos,
after all that, after before, never and maybe...after.

Suddenly

Suddenly he steps out on the veranda as if he'd
just appeared or had been there for a long time.
Maybe it's a veranda in some tropical country.
In the distance he can see the ocean. Now
he has become you, tall, dinner jacket, smoking,
your hair slightly gray, a small scar on your cheek.
Music from the Orchestra Baobab in the background
echoing through corridors from an empty ballroom.
Wrought iron grill, black and white tiles, the stars.
Maybe this is the moment you have been waiting for,
when the past catches up to the present and balances
over the future as if on the crest of a distant wave.
Such is the pleasure of looking at a print called
Smoking on a Veranda in Charleston, South Carolina.
The music is a tango, and you can't help thinking
slow, slow, quick-quick, slow. Suddenly you and your partner
look slightly away from each other, her gaze
over your shoulder, your gaze lost in the calligraphy
of tiles and columns, the wrought iron, the rooftops
of the shacks, the ocean beyond and of course,
the moonlight, because there is no suddenly
when your dancing partner just appears like that.
Place your left hand firmly against the small of her back.
Now remember something that never happened
like the poem you wrote while standing on the veranda,
the poem with the lilac scent of night-blooming jasmine.
Left foot first as you glide into another life,
with your partner in the white gown, backless.
Black, asymmetrical pearls around her throat, her hand lightly
on your shoulder. And that silver ring, with the unpolished
turquoise set on three prongs, you had it made for her
a long time ago, even though you're in no hurry
to ask her if she has a name yet.

Over

Over parapets of the Alhambra
over underground rivers
over qasidas of twisted cobras
over Gypsy knives and bandoliers
over blood-stained paving stones
over dogs howling in sandpaper wind
over olive trees weeping like willows
over the candied souvenirs of executioners
over the shadows of nuns on white-washed walls
over the mirrors wearing black
and the dead girl waiting on her veranda
over the green sky at dusk
and moonlight tangled in a froth of waterfall
over Sangre de Azteca tequila
and the screeching of traffic in the *zócalo*
over insomnia of the rooster weather vane
over papier-mâché skeletons over *gitarón*
trumpet twin violins guitar
over Tezcatlipoca and *la Virgen*
de la zona rosa and the three-eyed
silent woman of Tlatilco
over stolen codices feathered capes
handshakes and *abrazos*
over the high sacrificial peaks of snow
over taco joints roach coaches
nail-studded alleyways
where the gringos won't go
over a chest of American gold
to pay for the head of Pancho Villa
over pyramids diamond-etched

migrations of galaxies
over the wave that follows you home
over the pincers of the deadly *araña*
over a necklace of blue eyes
over names written on the rafters
over razor wires and checkpoints
over turrets and transparent minarets
over axes perfumed with sacrifice
over millstone calendars grinding nightmares
over charred trees of language
over mailboxes and through the rusty slot in the door
you came flying to land near my sad shoes
with your labyrinthine handwriting streaked with rain
with your stamps the color of midnight
you came flying.

Steady

Snakelike, the defaulting wind
longs to touch your face.
Along granite turrets I wait,
upright, without other embellishment.

The margin of sand and wind
etches a semblance of your face.
I accrue some worth in the wait.
Dawn is broke, without embellishment.

Rain bails out the wind.
Without expectations of your face
the fleet drops anchor and waits.
No sop no possum no embellishment.

Half of what I own belongs to the wind.
Half of what I remember I cannot face.
Armed in vinyl armor I wait.
Steady on course, my one embellishment.

Ledger

I am the heater with the rattling vent.
I am its raspy attempt at whisper.

The upright piano
that only has black keys, the one
that fell through the 6th floor
of the Gold Dust Hotel
and ended up on top of a mountain.

I am a tower on fire.
My name is Touch Little.
My stairway only goes down.

I am the margin defaulted.
The bank of earthworms.
Each earthworm riddling its way
through the same book.

I am the book, *Ledger of Domain.*

The horse-drawn moon.
The stars staggering home
after a night on the universe.

What snakelike amber,
what single thought bored in resin

are you? Magnifier. Your hands
haul in the dawn and cram it
into your genuine ostrich skin
briefcase. A classic. With two gussets.

Song for Ellas McDaniel

Bo Diddley Bo Diddley where you be?
Under the branches of the baobab tree.

Bo Diddley Bo Diddley what's your name?
Ask me again I'll tell you the same.

All the boys come Bo Diddley's house,
shoutin' and clappin' and jumpin' 'bout.

Hey Bo Diddley come out to play.
No fun playin' when you all alone.

Bo Diddley Bo Diddley got a violin.
Got a black cat bone got a rattlesnake skin.

Bo Diddley Bo Diddley Deputy Sheriff.
Hey Bo Diddley walk around heaven.

Bo Diddley Bo Dilley run for president.
Shave and a haircut, two bits.

Bo Diddley Bo Diddley made his own guitar
Bo Diddley Bo Diddley where you are?

Playin' my music in the stars
Playin' my music in the stars.

Hey! Bo Diddley.
Hey! Bo Diddley.

Hey Bo Diddley,
hey, Bo Diddley....

Cruel Students Give Distracted Professor Six Sestina Words

For a student she was without qualification,
although some considered her quixotic.
Her voice could cast a spell, mesmerize,
even when she screamed cacophonous
insults, making a morose paleontologist
feel suddenly small, like a leprechaun

hiding under a mushroom, a happy leprechaun.
If she smiled at you, without qualification,
your life was suddenly complete, a paleontologist
could dig you up and you'd be, like, quixotic,
deaf to all stress and the cacophonous.
Yes, she could please, charm, mesmerize

anyone, like that spellbinder, Franz Mesmer,
and he was dead—even that same leprechaun,
even if he was run over by a cacophonous
student driver, totally without qualification
for graduation. For a teacher, he was quixotic,
wearing his adventure fedora of a paleontologist.

Really, just the poetry professor, not a paleontologist.
The tilting of his student's cleavage, mesmerizing
Herr Professor, his attention a galloping Don Quixote
falling off the pale horse of indifference, leprechauned
by her upward glance, her smile of qualification
asserting: peace and maturity are cacophonous

monkeys in the monkey-mind cacophony.
But she did sonnetize: Dear Paleontologist,
I do like to look at you looking at my qualifications.
Cruel students threw the gauntlet of "mesmerize"
to befuddle their professor, added "leprechaun,"
and for good measure, threw in "quixotic."

Ha, they had said, Deal with it, Signor Professore, "quixotic,"
then try matching that with "cacophonous."
But being a poetic champion, he composed, like a leprechaun
almost avalanched, or a paleontologist
almost falling into a crevasse, mesmerized
by deep, musical, creamy qualifications.

He summoned a quixotic fellow, a paleontologist.
He ignored cacophonous but whispered mesmerizing.
He leapt like a leprechaun, no hesitation, no qualifications.

Mule Sestina

A mule is entirely nonpartisan
about the contents of its load.
The New Yorker, February 15th, 2010

To make a mule sestina
you need six words, well, five now.
Or is that four? How about imbroglio?
Or opposing meanings like cleave?
Your mule can be bucolic or frolic,
be listless or trot with enthusiasm.

Unlike a donkey, mules have enthusiasm,
like Professor Longhair at Tipitina's.
In Afghanistan, CIA mules frolicked,
but where are those mules now?
Tennessee's rejects did so cleave
to their mulish imbroglios.

Not for those mules Best in Show.
Some fell into deep chasms.
Unlike horses, mules cleave
to survival, not stubborn as a sestina
piling up words like a snowplow.
Not Darwinian—just pragmatic.

Francis, the mule, frolicked.
Sancho Panza's mule was El Rucio.
Perhaps not a name but for now
it'll do. A mule in its enthusiasm
carries 300 pounds. A mule sestina
carries 260 words, including cleave.

A parachuted mule will cleave
to the back of a plane, fake colic.
Sure it will carry rockets, concertina
wire, bullets, bandanas, meals-on-the-go,
and Stinger missiles with enthusiasm.
Mules are also in demand: the Dow

Jones is big on mule stock right now.
To a mare a donkey will cleave
even if it means faking orgasm.
But out of this manmade frolic
comes a mule. Sui generis as driven snow,
first and last of its kind—a mule sestina.

Time now for praise. How the mule will frolic,
and to living cleave. Not hinny, not beefalo,
not without enthusiasm, nonpartisan as a sestina.

Doll Heads

Doll heads are washing up on the beach.
They are bald, the bald heads of little babies
neatly severed from their torsos.

Did you, as a child, ever light a doll on fire?
Back in those days, dolls would burst into flame,
practically explode. There was a fuse-like

searing sound, and a smell, do you
remember the smell? Burning manikins
smell that way too, like glass burning.

Doll heads are discovered in trees.
No-one was seen placing them in the branches.

Doll heads can be found under pillows
and inside of small boxes. It has been surmised
that a person's head remains conscious

for one minute after decapitation.
I don't know, you'd have to ask the head.
If it is conscious, can it speak?

Insurgents have been beheading our people.
Barbaric, you say? Yes, I suppose so,
a kind of low-budget shock and awe.

A bomb crashes in on a restaurant.
Oops, our target was not there tonight.

The customers stand and dust off their clothes.
Some of the food is still edible.
Now the restaurant is outdoors.

Doll heads are drifting in with the tide.
Their little pates bobbing in the waves,
rolling a bit, coming to rest, some sideways

on one cheek, some face down, a few,
the lucky ones, looking up at the clouds.

Eyeglasses

The wire-rimmed eyeglasses of the commissar, repaired
with string, laid on an overturned ammunition box
after he signed an order for execution.

The eyeglasses Lincoln wore to the theater.
He was holding them just so, trying to make out the names
of the actors in *Our American Cousin,*
when suddenly he remembered the dream
he had the night before, and the night before that.

I can't prove it, but eyeglasses crawl
across the floor of any room where I am sleeping.

Jesus did not live long enough to need eyeglasses.

The pince-nez of Count Orlovsky.
The count lost them while hiding in the Opera House
during the uprising of the milkmen.
He longed for an earthquake.
How exquisite it would be, he thought,
if all five hundred crystal chandeliers
were to tremble at the same moment.

The eyeglasses Hitler wore as he wrote out his will in the bunker.
The diamond-studded lorgnette of Marie Antoinette.

Most eyeglasses resemble the exoskeleton
of the first eyeglasses to crawl out of the sea.

The man about to be executed by firing squad

was the childhood friend of the commissar.
He asked for his hat. He adjusted it just so.
He asked for his eyeglasses and put them on.
Then he shut his eyes.

God Creates the Universe

I'd like to write a poem about God
but it would have to be a poem written without words,
written without paper, written out of the silent spaces
between letters of the alphabet.
How boring, my poem about God.
Maybe in this poem God could have a job
like sweeping out the cafeteria at midnight.
There is God—he's an old guy on the night shift
who doesn't even know that he is God.
He sees a piece of paper on the floor
and stoops to pick it up.
It's a letter he wrote to himself
a long time ago, before the Big Bang, before
there were people who knew that he was God.
It says, Dear God, where are you? I have waited for you
so long but I can wait no longer. It is signed, Shekina,
your better half. God doesn't know what to make of this
but he puts the letter in his pocket, thinking
it might be important. He'll read it again
after he gets home. Here is God in my poem,
sitting in front of the TV watching reruns
of *Star Trek: The Next Generation.*
It is quiet because he has pressed the mute button
and, bathed in the flickering blue light,
he is beginning to fall asleep. But even
if he doesn't know it, he exists simultaneously
in this poem and in all time and space and beyond.
This very moment, God creates the universe.

Into the Forest

Branch over the shoulder, hobo branch.
First stick, whacker of enemies.
Stick of running away from home.
Divining branch of seeking, pathfinder.

First stick, whacker of enemies.
Branch fallen not far from the tree.
Divining branch of seeking, pathfinder.
Notched stick of crimson memory.

Branch fallen not far from the tree.
Buried branch of crossing rivers.
Notched stick of crimson memory.
Hoodoo branch exploding in flames.

Buried branch of crossing rivers.
Jesus, sharpened branch of the tree of David.
Hoodoo branch exploding in flames.
Stick scratching dirt of approaching battle.

Jesus, sharpened branch of the tree of David.
Serpent branch, guardian of crossroads.
Stick scratching dirt of approaching battle.
Bleeding branch of the Word of God.

Serpent branch, guardian of crossroads.
Branch of bodhi tree, branch of crucifixion.
Bleeding branch of the Word of God.
Alabama branch of the lynching tree.

Branch of bodhi tree, branch of crucifixion.
Chimpanzee stick of first tool, honeyed with termites.
Alabama branch of the lynching tree.
Flowering rod of Moses, branch of constellation.

Chimpanzee stick of first tool, honeyed with termites.
Forked stick, quivering at the thought of water.
Flowering rod of Moses, branch of constellation.
Branch over the shoulder, hobo branch.

Jesus Helped Me Make My Bed

As I was making my bed one evening
I looked up and there was Jesus.
He was not so tall as he looks on the cross.
And not as white-skinned either.
In fact, at first I thought it was Ari,
that crazy Moroccan I knew on Kibbutz Parode
who would kick the back of my chair
when he sat behind me at the movies.
Ari, who once dove in the swimming pool
the day they changed the water
and it was as clear as air. Actually,
it was air because it was empty.
Later I saw Ari with his head in bandages
and his arm in a sling. But Jesus
looked pretty good, considering
what he went through in that movie,
and how long he had been dead,
and how much energy it must have taken
to come back alive, and how out of shape
he must get sitting around heaven
all the time at the right hand of his dad.
So there was Jesus at the foot of my bed.
I wondered if I should fall to my knees,
but thought better of it. Frankly,
my heart was not in it and I thought
Jesus would know that. So I said,
Yehoshua, what do you want?
I thought it might impress him if I used
his real name. He did not answer
but began to help me make my bed.

He was pretty good at it too.
And soon my bed was professionally made
with tight hospital corners.
I began to wonder if I was dead
and wouldn't need to make my bed anymore,
or if the bed of my life was made
and it was time to lie in it, or if only
I made my bed this way every morning
would I live a better, more organized life?
I thought I was really getting somewhere
with this revelatory experience
but when I looked up, Jesus was gone,
as if the Eternal had burst into my room
and then was gone, like the time I punched the wall
on the kibbutz because Ari was laughing too loud
and it was three in the morning, and my fist
went right through the wall and into Ari's room
and that make him laugh even louder.
But it was so quiet where I was now.
No hole in my reality. Just me
and my bed so beautifully made
I would regret ever having to sleep in it.

Like Blowtorch

Let him not convince like blowtorch
or deconstruct a caress
that drips like a faucet.
That would be a conundrum,
a question for the wayfarer
and his two-step mambo.

Let her be mambo
to his blowtorch.
Destination to his way, fairer,
when day diminishes like a caress.
Sunset's end, the last conundrum
of problematic faucets.

They say she sighs like a faucet,
shimmies like mambo
to end all humdrums.
Like Dizzy he just blows
torching the harmonic caresses—
such a music, this wayfarer.

But she had gone way farther.
She had repaired the faucet
of faulty caresses.
They called her mambo-
crazy, a dancing blowtorch
incarnate, a shapely drum.

He and she, quite conundrum.
She and he wayfarers.
Both could love like blowtorch,
carry on like faucet,
twirl like mambo,
he and she folded, one caress.

Morning on eyelids does caress.
Empty bed so humdrum.
Where went the mambo?
Whither the way fairer,
leaving behind time's faucet
with the subtlety of a blowtorch?

Cold caresses illuminate the wayfarers.
Sheathed in conundrum, his heart, a leaky faucet.
Now she mambos in memory, like blowtorch.

Like, Awesome, Actually

Hitchhiking, I felt suddenly naked, you know?
As if the sum of my life was all, like,
See you later. But I'm not sure…uh,
maybe more like my clothes had actually
blown away, even my underwear. Bottom line—
caught in the back-draft of awesome.

Know what I'm saying? Awesome!
In the darkness, a semi's rear lights, you know,
reminded me of a skull. Bottom line,
I was afraid of something, like
a distant procession of torches actually
was crossing a bridge in hell, uh—

as if I were a detail in Hieronymus Bosch. Uh-
huh, that's right. Hitching is awesome.
Like a long take in a road-movie that actually
is the story of your life, or no,
just a life that is so much like
yours that it is yours, and the white line

down the highway is the time-line
of your fever, as if you had no skin, uh,
like flayed, so that even air hurts. It was like
my life could be summed up in an awesome
unfinished paint-by-numbers, you know,
like a painting found at a garage sale actually.

I began to construct a palace in my mind, not actually,
but some place where I could wander, sticking line-

by-line each pathetic memory, what little I know,
in columns and compartments, alcoves, uh,
or maybe a general store or a tower, all awesome
like a damn castle. I was standing all, like,

Duh…where am I, not paying attention, like
I wanted to get run over, when suddenly this Ferrari actually
stopped for me and there was this babe, awesome,
I mean totally Salma Hayek—bottom line:
goddess. Where ya going honey? she asked. I said uh…
and forgot, like, so then I said, I don't know.

It's like, I blew it, she drove off, that's the bottom line.
Like a fool actually, I just stood there, all still feeling…uh,
feeling awe. Some joy mixed with sad, mostly sad, you know?

Maria, the Figurehead from *La María Celeste*

She held a bouquet of pilot fish,
each one for sale, a token
for my lady, if I had a lady.

Being underwater she shed no tears
that I could see, besides, no one cared,
since she was not the Virgin Mary.

She was wrapped in seaweed
which I longed to untangle from
her body, her body mostly, well, all

torso, but what a torso. Torso of the bronze
Amazon. Torso of pallid Greek stone.
We severed anchor at midnight,

drifted out across the continental shelf.
Lucky I wore my fisherman's cap.
Her hair billowed, reminding me of you.

What you? How did you get in this poem?
Perpetual you of memory, you, a glimpse
in the turnstile of sunken subway,

just below the buried concrete slabs
where a stream that lost its name
trickles under a rusty grate.

Lucky me, the boys at the drowned public house
raised their grog to us, fare-thee-well,
me with the chaste torso leading me

into depths where even light would lose its way.

The Other *Odyssey*

Being of a certain age is like being Ulysses—
Ulysses, home at last, and the people
hate his guts for leading their young men
to the slaughter at Troy and returning alone
to murder the suitors, those who remained.
Ulysses, phah! they spit—sole survivor
with a mouth full of legends, no hero,
just a wily mortal with a bad reputation.
Being of a certain age is like being Ulysses
when Thetis, the sea goddess, avenges
the death of her son Achilles, whom Ulysses
tricked into going off to war. Ulysses
made to wander alone, carrying an oar,
for another ten years, to venture so far
from the ocean that some fool will ask,
What's that pole you're dragging,
a winnowing bat? Then and only then
can he turn toward home again.
That's the other Odyssey, the one
no poet writes about, the epilogue
better left forgotten. Here's Ulysses
sitting in a bar in some godforsaken hole
in Asia Minor surrounded by peasants, silent,
tired of hearing his own stories that even he
doesn't believe. He thinks of Calypso,
the way she'd come up behind him,
her small arms encircling his waist
while he stood staring at the sea.
Calypso, smiling in her sleep. Here's
Ulysses not thinking of Calypso,

turning his mind to the way everything,
the sand, the walls of the cave, the vault
of the stars, would rise and fall, waver
like the sea, like her breathing...

Mrs. Hightower Considers the Scissors

1.
She has always wondered if the scissors
are one object or two objects.
She holds the scissors up to the light.
Johnny Weissmuller slides under water,
a knife clenched between his teeth.
She places the point of one blade
on the faded envelope, unopened,
that lies on the marble table.
She twirls the other blade
in a circle around the stationary blade.
Mrs. Hightower says, I used to dance
like that, alone with the amber light
touching my white dress just so.
She grasps the blades in both hands
placing the handle holes over her eyes.
She's at the opera, in her private booth,
oblivious to the audience seated below.
The lights go dim, she sighs, reaches
into her silk purse and unfolds her lorgnette
to review the program. The lorgnette
was given to her by Mr. Hightower.
She loves the ivory and onyx handle
flecked with gold. Mrs. Hightower
places the scissors back on the table.
This is her favorite time of day. Soon it will be dark.

2.
The scissors were not born plural.
To sharpen themselves they repeat their name incessantly.

The scissors dance in a circle all alone.
The scissors only have two natural enemies.
The scissors want to dress in black and get taken to the opera.
The scissors open the door and you enter.
The cry of the scissors is the same as the cry of the night.
Slope-eyed scissors. Wall-eyed scissors. Scissors
with both eyes wide in disbelief. Winking scissors.
Scissors sliding, kicking, sliding gracefully across the floor.
One dice is a die but there is no name for one scissor.
I'm bored, say the scissors. I want to be confiscated.
I want to be Exhibit A. I want to be like the dawn
severing night from day. Scissors, cousin to the zipper.
Attracted to the magnet. Repelled by the magnet.
Hopelessly in love with the stone that fell from the sky,
the stone known only as, The Stranger. Siamese-twin scissors.
If the stone were to kiss only one blade, both blades would sigh.

Dragon of the Night Sky

The Great Serpent Mound in Ohio where the old ones
are sleeping. They will never wake up.

Marching towards the future we entered
the gates of Babylon, guarded by silent lions.

America, you a tar baby. Big baby. When I punch you
my fist sticks and you smile that tar baby smile.

The old ones in the Great Serpent Mound say:
we all have a husband or wife in the spiritual world.

America, are you Gilgamesh, risen from the land of death,
still in a rage, slaughtering the young men and women of Uruk?

The Great Serpent Mound, sister of Stonehenge,
brother to the constellation Draco, dragon of the night sky.

Ishtar cries out in pain, Enkidu rends the bull
from the hind quarters, its horns are bloody

like the drills and serrated blades of power tools,
like the eye sockets and severed limbs bleeding into the Tigris.

The Great Serpent Mound, sister of Stonehenge,
brother to the constellation Draco, dragon of the night sky.

The Great Serpent Mound, largest serpent effigy in the world.
Whoever built it was careful to crush all of their artifacts.

Last Words

What is the answer? What is the question?
Gertrude Stein

So you have come to the City of Questions.
Stop signs have no words, just question marks.
No answers here, but many allusions.
Can you go back? Maybe, maybe not.
You might ask someone a question:
Excuse me sir, where's the center of town?
He might answer with a question:
Why don't some birds have songs of their own?
Each person seems to know which way to go
even if all the street signs are empty.
But you fear that you will never know.
In days of old, this was known as maturity.
So you ruminate, rubbing your chin,
If there's no answer, what's the question?

After Tranströmer

There is a silent world
there is a crack
where the dead
are smuggled across the border.

There is a crack
in the mirror where motes of time
are smuggled across the border
between one glance and the next.

In the mirror where motes of time
lose their reflection
between one glance and the next.
Go ahead, see how moments

lose their reflection.
Stare at just one of your eyes,
go ahead, see how a moment
pauses when you turn away.

Stare at just one of your eyes
and not the other, one that
pauses when you turn away.
It is like that one evening

and not the other, one that
was like falling in slow motion.
It is like that one evening.
There is a silent world.

Onomatophobia

How much does one word weigh?
Cup, for instance.
If the word cup is full does it weigh more?
What if a word is full of God,
like the word enthusiasm?
Does enthusiasm weigh more than cup,
or the words shoe or spitball?
In Haifa, I saw all 300,000
words of the Torah etched
on the head of a pin.
Did the pin weigh more
than other pins?
When I sleep my hand slides
up and down my chest and belly,
or so I have been told.
Sometimes I dream that I have a zipper
running down the front of me.
Then I unzip myself and step out of my body.
According to Dr. Duncan MacDougall
of Haverhill, Massachusetts,
the me that steps out of me is my soul
and it weighs three-fourths of an ounce.
Just don't mention a certain word.
It is the word that weighs more than
all other words combined.
No, I won't tell you what it is.
And I have a note from my doctor
to back me up: I don't have to tell.
I also belong to an Onomatophobics
of America support group.

A certain word created the universe.
A certain word can destroy the universe.
If that word were a hole it would weigh
nothing, and everything would fall into it.
Stop! Listen! This is important.
This much I can tell you:
the word I fear most contains
the memory of hard candy.
Orange hard candy, sweet and bitter
as adolescence. Orange,
the word nothing rhymes with,
international safety orange,
orange vest, orange safety hat—
that's the color of the sky's weight
when the earth is on fire.

Yesterday's Word

Cajolery has a texture that is somewhat lacy,
like a slab of cheddar left in the microwave too long.
I jump over puddles in a year of much cajolery.

My wife does not appreciate cajolery
concerning the payment of bills.
Cajolery does sound rather jolly.

Let me be clear, cajolery is not lore of yore.
Not some royal earl with beads of coral, strumming his lyre.

It is as real as cola, darker than coal;
cloying, annoying, it always cajoles.
Some Carols do not care for it, they rale,
hiss, rattle, slosh and snort—

Cajolery, bah! But an eagle plunges from its aery
over the clear sea of cajolery,
where orcas leap and flail in relays of cajolery.

The Two

What a sunset. Don't you believe now?
Thus saith my companion on the beach walk.
Tired of waiting for an answer, the sky sets itself on fire.

A man and woman, fully dressed, stride out of the surf.
He is wearing a gray suit with a gray tie.
The monochromatic look. Very sharp.

She has on a spring dress, short, cut on the bias.
It swings with her hips like the ocean
tilting back and forth across the planet.

Neither appears to be wet.
My companion is tearful at God's sky.
The two arrived but were hardly noticed.

I saw them striding out of the waves
as if stepping off an escalator.
They seemed deep in some flirtatious conversation

and did not notice us standing on the beach
like the greeting committee. Of course,
when I say we, or us, I mean myself.

It Said

It said write your whole name four times, in four lines—that will be your first stanza. The second stanza, just write down some names from today's obituaries. Cool, you added, and then write down the names of everyone we know who has died. You, being my Chinese girlfriend just returned from a trip. I was happy to see you and was kissing you on the cheek. Then I was carrying you down the hall, telling you my dream. You were still my Chinese girlfriend, thin, easy to carry, your black hair in a bob. Damn, I said. What's wrong, you asked. If this is a dream, I replied, well, you could be someone else, like maybe Salma Hayek. Don't be silly, you said. Now you were you, my wife, not Chinese, still back from a trip, your suitcases open on the living room floor. You were standing there naked, except for your cowboy boots, as you modeled, one after the other, some dresses you bought. I approved. Then I was a child in a classroom. You were the teacher I would grow up and marry someday. It was late, everyone else had gone home. I was just finishing up writing one hundred times on the blackboard: I shall love my life…I shall love my life.

Under the Constellation of the Lyre

Under the constellation of the lyre I broke my lyre.
Stupid lyre, reminding me of a journey I had not taken.
Reminding me of a swan, and I don't care for swans either.

I, who had received a special delivery, registered,
empty envelope. And that mail lady, the slender one,
with the tomboy saunter, where had I seen her before?

At night I console myself by asking myself questions.
Why did the moon depart so suddenly? Here, incidentally,
is the part of the poem where his wife enters with his scarf.

But I was already departed, gone on a journey,
drifting down a long stairway, with my hands folded
over my chest politely, like little wings in prayer.

I could not help but notice all the broken plates and glasses
I had dropped or thrown in my life, embedded in the wall,
and the lost keys and my missing collection of matchbooks:

The Farmer's Daughter, The Kiss and No-tell, The Alibi Room.
Here is the place where twenty-six lines are missing
from the manuscript, perhaps an image for time wasted.

But we can assume that the speaker of the poem opened his eyes
but remained deep in sleep. That the dream proceeded on its own,
despite the narrator's abrupt departure, and the absence of moonlight.

Acknowledgments

Grateful acknowledgment is made to the editors of the following journals, anthologies and websites, where versions of these poems first appeared:

13 Miles from Cleveland: "Falling Pattern."

American Poetry Journal: "Gacela of the Mutant Jellyfish," "Gacela of Paper" and "Yesterday's Word."

Barn Owl: "The Boxes."

Barrow Street: "The Other Odyssey."

Big City Lit: "A Play for Finger Puppets in Five Acts."

Center: "Gacela of Noon."

diode: "Japanese Scientists" and "Onomatophobia."

Georgia Review: "The White Ghosts."

In Posse Review: "Doll Heads" and "Thomas."

Más Tequila Review: "Gacela of the Grey Stone," "Over" and "Self Portrait as *Two Fridas*."

Other Voices International Project: "Into the Forest."

The Pedestal: "Saudade."

Poemeleon: "Like, Awesome, Actually" and "A Poem by Kit Loney."

Pool: "After."

Praxilla: "Mystical Journey with Commands" and "Onomatophobia."

Qarrtsiluni: "Gacela of Paper."

Rattle: "A Poem by Andy Rooney."

Redactions: "Maria, the Figurehead from La María Celeste."

South85: "The Only Story I Know" and "Red Wing."

Sugar House: "Dangerous Journeys and the Wizard Oz" and "Trout Dreams."

Waccamaw: "Either/Or and Favorite Movies."

Writers At Work: "God Creates the Universe."

"Into the Forest" appeared in *Seeking: Poetry and Prose Inspired by the Art of Jonathan Green*, edited by Kwame Dawes and Marjory Wentworth, published by The University of South Carolina Press. "Under the Constellation of the Lyre" appeared in the anthology *Don't Blame the Ugly Mug*, edited by Steve Ramirez and Ben Trigg, published by Tebot Bach. "The White Ghosts" appeared in *The Southern Poetry Anthology Volume I*, edited by Stephen Gardner and William Wright. "With No One to Guide Us" appeared in *Kakalak Anthology of Carolina Poets 2008*, edited by Richard Allen Taylor, Beth Cagle Burt, and Lisa Zerkle, published by Main Street Rag.

And thanks also to the fellowship of The Long Table Poets of Charleston, South Carolina.

About the Author

Richard Garcia is the author of *The Flying Garcias* from University of Pittsburgh Press, *Rancho Notorious* and *The Persistence of Objects*, both from BOA Editions, and a chapbook of prose poems, *Chickenhead*, from FootHills Publishing. His poems have appeared in *The Georgia Review*, *Crazyhorse*, *Ploughshares*, *Pushcart Prize XXI* and *Best American Poetry*. A collection of prose poems, *The Chair*, will be published by BOA in the fall of 2014. He teaches in the MFA in Creative Writing Program at Antioch University Los Angeles, and lives on James Island, SC.